CONVERSION AND IDENTITY:
The Pastoral Care and Discipleship of Converts from Islam in the Context of the UK

I0895790

CONVERSION AND IDENTITY:
The Pastoral Care and Discipleship of Converts from Islam in the Context of the UK

Saira Malik

Copyright © Saira Malik 2022

First published 2022 by Regnum Books International

Regnum is an imprint of the Oxford Centre for Mission Studies
St. Philip and St. James Church, Woodstock Road, Oxford, OX2 6HR, UK
www.regnumbooks.net

09 08 07 06 05 04 03 8 7 6 5 4 3 2 1

The right of Saira Malik to be identified as the author of this work has been asserted by her in accordance with the Copyright, Designs and Patents Act 1988.

All rights reserved. No part of this publication may be reproduced, stored in a retrieval system, or transmitted, in any form or by any means, electronic, mechanical, photocopying, recording or otherwise, without the prior permission of the publisher or a license permitting restricted copying. In the UK such licenses are issued by the Copyright Licensing Agency, 90 Tottenham Court Road, London W1P 9HE.

British Library Cataloguing in Publication Data
A catalogue record for this book is available from the British Library

ISBN: 978-1-5064-9754-9
eBook ISBN: 978-1-5064-9755-6

Typeset in Palatino by Words by Design

Cover image by Sunguk Kim, www.unsplash.com

Distributed by Fortress Press in the US, Canada, India, and Brazil

regnum

Hikma Partnership
researching, writing, creating and sharing

Dedication

To the memory of Gulshan Esther, who assisted me in my early discipleship path.

Acknowledgements

I would like to thank the individuals who generously gave their time to this research, without whom this work could not have been completed. Your invaluable input has helped formulate some key findings. I would also like to express my gratitude to Dr M Barnes SJ for his careful attention to the study and helpful advice during my studies, especially the writing of the thesis on which this book is based.

I add my thanks to the Hikma Research Partnership for facilitating adapting my MA thesis to be suitable for publication in book form. In addition, my thanks to Elizabete Santos and Tony Gray of Regnum Books for their work on the production processes.

FOREWORD AND SERIES PREFACE

Pat Brittenden, Jonathan Andrews and Paul Bendor-Samuel, Series Editors

This is the first book in a series entitled *Global Voices of a Muslim Background* being prepared by the *Hikma Partnership* and published by Regnum Books. The series seeks to enable the global church to be enriched by hearing from those of Muslim heritage. In addition, it seeks to enable such people to become authors. What are we learning from one another? How are the diversity of backgrounds and varied experience of Christ informing us all?

We are delighted that Saira Malik is one of the first contributors to this series. Her work examines what we regard as key themes from this part of the global body of Christ and its active acceptance and participation within the worldwide church. What are the challenges to people's sense of identity as their move from one faith tradition to another, becoming members of the body of Christ? From these flows what sort of support might they need. Saira makes the point that contexts vary and no two people experience the journey to Christ and becoming members of his church in the same way.

It is our desire with this series to enable more such people to become active participants in Christ's mission, enriching the global church in the process.

Hikma Partnership

researching, writing, creating and sharing

Contents

PREFACE

This book is based on my dissertation written in 2012 for my MA in Christianity and Interreligious Relations at Heythrop College, part of the University of London. The dissertation was based on interviews with two groups of people, namely converts from Islam and those supporting such people. There were 22 interviewees in total. The interviews were recorded to allow for academic assessment of the research methods used and the accuracy of my recording and analysing the findings. The recordings were duly deleted after the assessment had been completed.

All the candidates were known to me. The candidates represent a diverse range of Christian denominations. The converts are disciples who have followed their discipleship paths for over 10 years. The converts are from South Asia, Africa and Iran. It would be correct to state that 90% of these converts were never deeply embedded in Islam. A majority of those who have cared for converts have been in ministry for over 20 years and include church leaders. Many of the interviewees have been involved in the formation of the Church's understanding of mission in multi-faith contexts. They also have a wealth of experience, not just in the UK, but as missionaries in Muslim countries.

I am a convert from Islam, hence my interest in the subject of conversion and identity. Furthermore, I desire to share the complex discipleship paths of people like me that will enable the wider Church to understand and support our brothers and sisters out of Islam better and help them grow and flourish in the body of Christ.

I am delighted to make my findings available more widely in this book.

Chapter One – Introduction

The Significance of the Issue

In the ever-increasing literature about conversion and identity, an interesting direction is taken by author and Episcopal priest Paul-Gordon Chandler when he asks "how Christ could become 'naturalized' in the Islamic context" (Chandler, 2007:2). Chandler meets Arab Syrian novelist and writer Mazhar Mallouhi, who talks about a gradual adjustment from Islam to the community of Christ. He speaks of conversion as a process of "transformation not rupture" (p117).

Mallouhi is presented here as an alternative approach to the traditional ways in which conversion has been viewed, and also as a challenge to Christians. He is the voice of a convert who is living out his Christian faith whilst residing in his indigenous culture and managing all the issues that interculturation brings. These involve dialogical encounter, mutuality and enrichment through transformation. His journey has been difficult, often misunderstood; however, Christians can learn invaluable lessons from it.

Mallouhi is a follower of Jesus who has presented Him in "culturally acceptable" terms, in order to eliminate Islamic misunderstandings of the Gospel and Jesus. He avoids debates, instead seeking commonalties, and focuses on Jesus. He wants Muslims to experience "authentic" Christian friendships without "ulterior" agendas, and for everything to be left with God (p52). He honours Muslims, respecting their tradition, communities and culture. Mallouhi's ultimate vision is one of bridging the divide between Islam and Christianity. His approach has been identified with the "Insider Movement". I will critique the "Insider" approach in the final chapter.

Mallouhi encourages "Muslim disciples of Jesus" to continue with their old tradition's way of life and devotional practice like, for example, in the manner of their prayer. He feels many "natural Christians" or "insiders" successfully follow Christ never needing to interact with the Christian community, living in the cultures in which God has placed them (p123). The "insiders" attend small fellowships, and have adapted Islamic tenets, rituals, worship and religious days to have new meanings. He feels that Muslim disciples of Jesus are "culturally" Muslims and "spiritually" Christ's followers, and following Jesus "enhances their true identities", rather than denying who they were (p107).

What have other thinkers written about converts from Islam? JM Gaudeul is a scholar of Arabic and Islamic Studies who has lived amongst converts from Islam, recording their journeys and experiencing their discipleship paths for himself. In this regard, he is an excellent precursor to my study. He encourages Christians to analyse these journeys of self-discovery, in order for the Church to be equipped to better understand their needs. The Church belongs to all, no one owns it. According to Gaudeul, new disciples require their admittance and acceptance (Gaudeul, 1996:293).

Gaudeul asks, why would a Muslim want to convert to Christianity? His main research findings point to the reasons for Christian conversions as:

- the attractiveness of Christ
- thirst for "truth"
- salvation certainty
- seeking community
- forgiveness
- experiences of God in prayer and
- a significant calling from God

Gaudeul suggests the aspects that most attracted Muslims were "Christians who welcomed them, Christians who radiated their faith in an admirable character and lifestyle, a community that "felt like home", and enjoyment of singing and celebration" (p147). These aspects, as we shall see, resonate with the many Islamic and cultural concepts that the converts in my study have grown up with in their tradition. Converts also express a preference for the New Testament view of God. Here God is portrayed as loving, protective, God the Father. In Islam, although God has many different names that speak of His character, He can appear "remote, angry, a tyrannical figure to be obeyed blindly" (Warraq, 2003:92).

Gaudeul emphasises that Jesus plays a central role in the conversion of Muslims; he has attracted them, fascinated them and spoken to them in a very direct way. Gaudeul speaks of Muslims who have never read any Christian theology calling out to Jesus in times of deep distress and encountering Him; later they were guided by the Holy Spirit to "know" Jesus for themselves. He states that "the reality of God goes far beyond any human culture" (p8) and he suggests that "the presence of "dissidents" who choose a religious alternative is a sign of a healthy society" (p18). He reinforces Mallouhi's views when he states that there are many nameless Muslim believers living in their communities, who have never crossed into a Christian church, who follow Jesus.

Gaudeul observes that the conversions of those he researched were gradual, having taken entire lifetimes. He cites Zohra, a Lebanese woman, who is a Christian but "culturally" is "fully Muslim". Zohra states "Islam is not a body of doctrine in opposition to the Christian faith, but a movement towards God" (p121). She feels her conversion is a fulfillment of her previous religious life, and a means of preparing her for what lies ahead. Gaudeul suggests more converts are trying to live in a way that does not involve a "rupture" with their culture and families, and he stresses that a Christian convert from Islam is not "making new recruits"; they are present as witnesses of a meeting with the living God: they have been chosen. In his view, this is not something that can be manufactured, it is there for all to see, and the rest is up to God.

I suggest, after researching conversion to and from Islam, that misunderstanding surrounds convert groups. However, converts should be heard as they understand the perspectives of both traditions, and are potential agents for cross-cultural dialogue and mediation. The studies discussed above served as the starting point for my own work.

Guidelines for the Care of Converts

The need for specific guidance in the care of converts from Islam has arisen from various factors:

- The increasing number of churches with significant numbers of people of other faiths.
- The increasing number of people from other faith backgrounds coming to Christian faith.
- The need to encourage a public and church culture in which mature and considered conversion (from and to any faith) is

seen as a normal aspect of human growth and development in a society which values both freedom of expression and a critical approach to religion and belief.

- The need to provide appropriate ways for local churches to nurture new Christians from other faith backgrounds. This has to do with the wellbeing and growth in the faith of new Christians. This requires ensuring that leaders and congregations have the necessary understanding to welcome them, with a wider appreciation by churches of the relationship between the Gospel and culture. I desire a more confident and widespread public commitment to the principle of freedom of religious conscience.

The Church of England has always stressed reaching out to those of other faiths. Anglican priest Guy Wilkinson describes this in terms of the Church's mission of "hospitality" and "embassy". He explains that "*Generous love,* the Anglican Interfaith theology, speaks of 'embassy' and 'hospitality', two 'heart' movements of the mission of God. 'Embassy', which is about Christian ambassadors proclaiming the Good News of the Kingdom, comes as the consequence of the loving nature of God, expressed in the life, death and resurrection of Jesus and the work of the Holy Spirit. 'Hospitality', is the welcome and openness that is the heart of God, who is love. Both these movements should be observable in the life of Christian communities" (Wilkinson, 2009:15). These words need to become a living reality for churches welcoming new disciples of Jesus from Islam.

My book's overarching theoretical framework focuses on the themes of conversion and identity. It will record and analyse the experiences of converts from Islam to Christianity, and those who care for converts, in respect of their own discipleship paths and the handling of pastoral care in the UK. The converts and those who care for converts are independent groups, with pseudonyms being used to identify them. They were interviewed with a series of open-ended questions designed to elucidate their personal journeys.

From this initial discourse, one challenging question raised by my study is what is the level of understanding of identity issues amongst converts and those who care for them? I will answer this question throughout the study from different perspectives. I suggest that, as we progress through the study, we will be able to underpin an explanation or hypothesis for the phenomena observed. My research makes no claims to being "scientific" in the sense often associated with quantitative studies. Rather, I make qualitative observations that serve to answer my hypothesis. My hypothesis is that Muslim converts from Islam are taken on a different "straight path" which, because it focuses on a personal relationship with Christ, embraces all the emotional, intellectual and cognitive highs and lows of any intense intimate relationship.

CHAPTER TWO – THE STORIES

In this chapter I will present the highlights of the journeys and experiences of both converts who have embraced Christianity and those who have undertaken the care of such people. The material is presented thematically based on the interview questions used. We will meet the converts first, followed by those who supported them.

The names of all the converts are pseudonymised.

The converts' faith journeys vary not least because they were raised in a variety of settings. There are, though, some recurring themes. I trust that you enjoy meeting some of my friends.

CONVERT ACCOUNTS

First question: *What was the key moment in your conversion?*

Amina is a Catholic. When she was very young she had "a puzzling yet vivid dream of her father taking her mother and her to a Catholic church and leaving Amina there". She tried to take her own life as a young adult and "heard a voice telling her she had no right to do so". She was unsure about these experiences at the time but later came to understand their significance.

Mehrdad shared a room with a Christian boy at college and they became good friends. As his friend spoke about his faith, so Mehrdad came to feel that God could be the answer for his future, as his earthly father had forsaken him.

Fatima remembers feeling that Jesus is a "gentle Prophet" and someone to listen to. She was baptised after she realised that she "needed peace and that Jesus was the answer".

Hadiza had a powerful encounter with God. She was broken after a bad relationship. She called to God to ask Him if He was real. She felt His hand on her head, "a strong power went through her, a light appeared in the room and she felt God's peace and reassurance". She described it as "being enveloped in a pool of love, with God cradling her as a Father would a child".

Hamza felt that Jesus was answering his prayers and was told that the love God had for him is "a deep, special and unconditional love". This spurred him on to study the Gospels, feeling that there was some "truth" in them, for him.

Maryam felt the Holy Spirit prompting her when she heard a sermon on the "God-Man Jesus" and felt that "God was challenging her in some way".

The other four converts described their key moments in conversion as being when they were studying the Bible either on their own or with others.

Second question: *What were key moments in your journey of faith?*

Amina remembers that her baptismal classes were important, as also were the times she spent with other Christians. She stated that "I felt part of a community, part of a large family" amongst her Catholic friends. Her first Christmas as a believer was very significant because she felt at "home" and knew that following Jesus was going to change her life forever.

Mehrdad started to walk in step with the Holy Spirit, allowing guidance from the Spirit, often not worrying about which country he would be in and where he would find work. He went to a church in London which was undergoing a revival and this rekindled a strong passion for God within him. When "asked to move and go" by God, Mehrdad felt "a sense of empowerment which has got easier over the years". He described the strength from the Lord Jesus that he has gained over time and the wisdom of the Lord guiding him through difficult decisions.

Fatima experienced many highs and lows on her faith journey. She had bouts of depression in the early years and her faith was challenged by her illness. She sympathises with her church and remembers at the time that they did not understand her needs.

Hadiza had a constant friend on her journey, who was a "messianic Jew". When Hadiza's father died, she got back in touch with her estranged family but did not tell them about her conversion. She felt that she was in touch with "her roots" when she joined a South Asian church but this did not last. Finally, she came to a church with people from many ethnic backgrounds, and felt that this church would be "her family". It was here that she felt the call for ordination. She states "I had already seen myself sitting outside a cathedral with a white collar on" years before she made this decision.

Hamza came from an ethnically mixed home; his mother was Christian and his father was Muslim. His mother had prayed for one of her sons to become a Christian. His father was angry when he started to study the Bible. Hamza had a wonderful experience in church, describing it as a "moment of peace and a burden lifted from him" and decided that this was the "right path for him". Once Hamza had converted and left home, his faith caused disputes between his parents. Hamza finally told his father that he had been baptised; his father's response included violence. He describes that he "was dead to his father" after this point.

Maryam's conversion was helped by a Christian teacher, who gave her an English-language Bible. This made a significant impact, as up to that point she had only read the Quran in Arabic and Urdu. Her five daily prayers (*salat*) had always not had much resonance with her and she had questioned their validity and relevance. Today she prays to Jesus as she would talk to a friend and feels the Lord's presence during her prayer times.

The other four converts stated their key journey moments as times when they were nurtured and mentored by Christians.

Third question: *When did you "feel most at home" in your new faith?*

Amina felt at home when she was being cared for by her godparent, who was her "sponsor" at her baptism. She had Catholic friends in her social circle and "felt included".

Mehrdad felt at home when he was "walking closely in step with the Holy Spirit and felt the presence of God in his life". He saw the faithfulness of God when he was in need and knew that "God would not fail him".

Fatima felt at home when she joined a church which had Iranian Christians, and whilst she was forming her "new identity in Christ" with the help of her pastor.

Hadiza felt at home when she fully understood her call to ordination.

Hamza felt at home when he was empowered to "find his new spiritual path for himself". He was cared for by his minister, stating that his pastor was "like an ideal older brother to me".

Maryam did not feel at home for a number of years and this was because the "churches she was attending did not understand her culturally". She left home when she was very young and eventually met a Christian family who became "like an adopted family", where "she felt loved and supported".

The other four converts described "feeling most at home in their new faith" when they felt that they could clearly see why they were following Jesus and understood their calling within God's purposes.

Fourth question: *What support did you receive?*

Amina outlined a very ordered way in which she was supported within the Catholic tradition. She went through the Rite of Christian Initiation for Adults (RCIA), the standard process by which an adult formally joins the Roman Catholic Church. She would regularly meet with her priest, going to church most Sundays. She would have "deep conversations" with Catholics, who she felt "did not judge her in any way". She was never made to "feel like a convert" and was assimilated easily into her church.

Mehrdad felt that he was encouraged to adopt a "disciplined approach to his faith early on" and allowed to ask as many questions as he felt he needed to. He went on to take responsibility for many things that his church was involved in, including street outreach. Such activities allowed him to grow in his faith and witness.

Fatima was fortunate to have many Christians around her who both prayed for her and advised her. She joined a Bible study group which she later began to lead.

Hadiza had a difficult time settling into one church; importantly, she felt she had the freedom to explore many options. Finally, she stayed in one church, stating "they modelled for me on what it meant to be a Christian".

Hamza states that his minister had "the knowledge of a great scholar and a heart of a good shepherd". Hamza had a great deal of respect for him and he clearly was a positive role model.

Maryam felt her innermost needs were fulfilled. She was blessed with a physical new family, and a Church family, together with somewhere to live.

Inaya found settling in one church difficult, due to her not fully understanding how her life was changing and not being sure about "her identity in Christ". She tried to explain this to the churches, but there was a clear lack of understanding. Eventually, she ended up going to a home church "where she could just be herself".

All the converts felt that they received good biblical teaching. For the other three converts interviewed, their churches did provide practical reflection and support on the issues that they were facing with their families and communities.

Fifth question: What difficulties did you face?

Amina felt she needed challenging about the new concepts she was being taught. For example, how did she feel about the Trinity, the communion of saints,[1] the role of Mary, questions about pro-life and contraception? She also was not fully prepared for how to give her "testimony" of her conversion. When she was asked to do so, she felt caught off-guard and unprepared because she was unclear about what was expected of her.

Fatima's biggest issue was telling her family about her conversion. She was concerned about her prospects of getting married. Fortunately, she met her Christian husband in the UK and it was her church that introduced them.

Hadiza stated that, surprisingly for her, she found the South Asian Church the least helpful in her pastoral care. She feels that her current journey is a hard, costly and lowly one. Having effectively been "cut off from her family", she feels she needs loving support in her ongoing journey.

Hamza had doctrinal challenges to deal with about the Trinity, which did get resolved. He also had not so much a difficulty, but a concern, to see "evidence of the practical out-workings of the Christian faith". In other words, people's faith in action and in the reality of their daily lives.

Maryam states that she regrets "losing the cultural identity she had and untangling herself from it". Since those early years she has come to an understanding that converts need to hold on to the values in their traditions that enrich their new faith journeys. Maryam and others need time and support to evaluate what of their past traditions is compatible with their new-found faith in Christ, and what has to be rejected as unbiblical. This process is rarely easy.

Inaya found it particularly difficult to seek help, feeling a sense of powerlessness. The "culturally sensitive" mentors she needed

---

[1] A phrase in the Nicene Creed and hence widely used in Catholic churches, as well as within other Christian traditions.

were just not there. She felt her difficulties arose from the "misunderstandings of the church about her faith journey" and how to find ways to help her.

The other three converts questioned had initial difficulties around doctrinal understanding, which did get resolved. An exception to the general pattern was **Mehrdad,** as he did not state any difficulties. To use a technical term, he was an outlier, that is, someone with a different view from the consensus.

Sixth question: *How did you transition from the old faith to your new faith – was it sudden or gradual? Please explain how this took place for you.*

Amina felt that Islam was "not deeply embedded in her thinking" and so her transition was less problematic and gradual. She did have issues with the idea of the communion of saints, as "it felt odd for her", but since then she has come to a better understanding of this. She never had any issues with the veneration of Mary, or any significant doctrines.

Fatima felt "liberated" and was "ready to embrace Christianity" and for her it was sudden: she was an outlier for this question.

Hadiza also described her transition as "liberation" from the ritual practices of her old tradition, but it was gradual.

Maryam feels she "spiritually transitioned" suddenly, praying to God "as her Father", but states her mental and emotional transition was gradual. She did hold on to some ingrained cultural concepts. One of these was "honour/ shame" thinking. This will be discussed in chapter three.

Inaya was also an outlier for this question. She had the most challenges in her transition. She continues to pray in the same way she did previously and covers herself, reading the Quran regularly and visiting the mosque. Inaya stated that she has "genuinely been struggling with her new identity", trying to hold on to the old whilst discovering the new.

The other five converts questioned had a sincere wish to transition to their new faith. They accepted the doctrinal teachings and regularly attended church, and slowly adapted to the manner of prayer, worship and sermon formats.

Having met the converts and listened to a summary of their stories we now meet some people who seek to support people who choose to become disciples of Jesus. Most are from a Christian background; two, though, are converts from Islam.

Accounts of Those Responsible for the Care of Converts, Including Church Leaders

As before, I will use a question-and-answer format.

First question: *how did you accompany the convert on their journey, how did you meet, in what context?*

Peter knew some converts from the asylum cases he was handling. He admitted that initially "he had some sceptical reservations about this". He would see individuals in church or at their homes. The conversations were "open and warm". He tried to tell their families when they were thinking about conversion and "never emphasised baptism too early".

Esther used to go to the home of the convert she cared for and prayed with both him and his Christian wife, as part of her pastoral visits.

Simon knew the Christian relative of the convert he looked after. Simon stated "he was a young boy who had lost a regular sense of fatherhood in his life". He would meet him every Friday, with the initial talks being quite broad; they were "about lessons he needed for life, about human relationships".

Mark met some of his converts during door-to-door work he started some 20 years ago. Mark met this one boy after school and gave him homework lessons. He felt "this boy had issues with adults because some had abused his trust" but slowly the boy asked questions about Christianity. The Holy Spirit began to work and soon he came to faith in Christ. Mark adopted this boy "like a son" and he remarked that "he looked upon me as his father". The boy never came to church because he was fearful of his community. Mark would speak with him whenever he could and eventually the young man moved out of the city and married a Muslim girl.

Martha regularly met converts at various locations, including her home, in the park and in cafes. She was told about these people by church members who then put her in touch with them.

Abdullahi (who is a convert from Islam himself) got to know a Wahhabi man he met one day. The man was an academic and their engagements were "thought-provoking". They studied both the Bible and Quran and the "idea of unity with Christ appealed to this man". He became a Christian after one year of regular contact and discussion.

Luke met his convert, who was a refugee, when the man turned up on his doorstep having been introduced to Luke by a Christian.

John met his convert after they were introduced by the man's landlord. He spoke very little English. He had been divorced from his Muslim wife. He had run for his life from the place where he became a Christian and sold his land back home, with no idea of where his life was going. He had been in Pakistan, Turkey and Iran, smuggling himself into the UK on a lorry. He needed a lot of practical help initially: he had no money and needed somewhere to live, which John organised for him. John took him to a multi-cultural church, where he was comfortable.

Ayuba (who is a convert from Islam herself) was introduced to the convert that she cared for when the church that had tried to provide support realised that they were struggling to meet her needs.

Stephen and his wife Sarah met a lady who was studying in the UK. They became good friends, meeting her at their home and she eventually went to church quite naturally with them. She attended an Alpha course, having never stepped inside a church before. Stephen also helped this lady with her asylum case.

Stephen and his wife also looked after a young boy, helping him with his asylum appeal. Stephen even visited the boy's family back home to assure them not to worry, as he had left his own country fearing for his life. They "shared in both his rejoicing and his upsets". They were introduced to him by a Christian relative of his. Fortunately, they both could speak his language, which helped immensely.

Second question: *Please explain your lines of experience? What went well and what went badly?*

Peter felt the struggles that converts underwent "had given them a deeper faith than many other disciples of Christ he knew". Peter feels if Christians come alongside converts in their early years, ensuring they receive regular fellowship, then converts will often mature into disciples that have a "strong passion for Christ and for witnessing for Him". In his church, a ministry to Iranians has specially helped the converts from Iran. He feels Iranians "tend to be self-sufficient, consulting with him occasionally". Unfortunately, he has seen Christians enthusiastically "expecting too much of converts too soon" and this has meant that "some have drifted away, sadly".

Esther's overall experience with the convert she met was positive. He was very inquisitive and had many questions on his heart. She felt he had a "spiritual hunger". He came to the church very easily and got involved. He "felt at home" there, as the environment was multi-cultural. She recalls that he felt there was "peace in the church and amongst the worshippers".

Simon worked through a course based on John's Gospel with the young boy. He discussed God and His character with him. Simon tried to get the boy to think for himself and discern his own path. Simon feels that "spoon feeding is not, in principle, a good way of caring for converts". The important thing was to teach "how to understand the word of God and how to apply it in your life". Simon felt the young boy bonded well with him and "treated him like a father". The young boy could not biblically always understand certain things. For example, "freedom in Christ" did not mean "free to do anything we wanted, including to sin". He also found getting connected to people challenging in his church, falling victim to the Western individualistic culture and not the more "communal" approach he was used to.

Mark felt that "God was there right from the beginning" in his relationship to this boy. He came to him distressed and their bond grew and they began to talk in a "deeper way". Mark states "they all became a family together". Mark did have a few difficulties, on the part of Asian Christians who spoke about the boy to the Muslim community, feeling they "should not have endangered him in this way".

Martha worked through courses designed for new believers with her convert contacts. Martha emphasised the need for converts to meet other Christians, and not become dependent on her. She encouraged them "to be part of the life of the church". She felt converts do better when they are not pushed too much and that Christians need to be patient with them.

Luke had a real struggle with the man he was taking care of. He needed a translator and he did not have written materials in his language to give him. The convert had suffered a great deal of persecution because of his conversion, so Luke "really needed to show him the love and trust he craved". Luke persevered and got him an MP3 of the New Testament in Urdu. He regularly went to Luke's home and has made it his own.

John provided practical help to the man he cared for in any way that he could. He also had one-on-one Bible studies with him. John stated "he became more uninhibited and bolder in his faith, and felt at ease praying, which he had struggled with initially".

Ayuba was always "there as a listening ear" for the lady she was looking after. Ayuba understood the excitement of finding something new in Jesus and wanting to share this with others, as she saw this convert become bolder in her witness. However, Ayuba stated "she wanted her safety and I was very protective of her".

Stephen and his wife "opened their door" to the lady that they looked after. The church they attended also cared for her and her son. She went to a Farsi-speaking home group and Stephen's wife would have a one-on-one Bible study with her. Stephen feels "being a Christ-like role model" for a convert is as important as Bible studies and structured approaches. Stephen stated that "she is Christ's disciple not ours", admitting that we need to remember to let go and allow God to work in a person's life. Some things went badly, notably when her estranged husband was not happy with her baptism, which resulted in her divorce. Stephen admitted that this was a difficult time, but they had to trust that she was making the right decisions in her life.

Third question: *Please describe "theology of conversion".*

Peter and **Luke** stressed "it is not a religion that the disciple is coming into but a relationship with God", together with "letting go of the old and coming into the new".

Stephen explained his understanding of conversion theologically, "as a process whereby a person is born again in Christ, receiving new life and the presence of God in their lives by His Spirit. At the core of this process lies a new allegiance to Jesus as Lord and a new worldview. If this allegiance is allowed to influence that person's habits, decision-making, behaviour and relationships, this eventually brings about a gradual but radical transformation in the person, which is noticed by others. Over the years the conversion continues gradually making the person more like Christ".

Fourth question: *How did you help the convert adjust to their new reality? What could they take with them or leave behind?*

Peter avoids anything "process-driven" and feels that converts are individuals; each have their own paths that they need to take. He wants converts in his church to form a fellowship, but not be separated from the main Church. In this closer network, he feels common issues can be raised, and the guidance they need sought.

Simon feels that converts do not always experience a reality that they should in our churches. They need to fully experience a "living kingdom reality" that Christians are "committed to being sacrificially there for them". Simon quotes from the Bible from (1 Corinthians 9:20) "to the Jews I became like a Jew". He implements the Quran in teaching converts and uses "Islamic concepts that Muslims understand such as the idea of ritual sacrifice and holy days" and applies this thinking into the new contexts of the Bible, to help converts understand "similar" Christian concepts.

Martha ensured the young man understood the Christian view of the concepts of prayer and fasting and how these are carried out. Major events like birthdays, Easter and Christmas are celebrated as "the new festivals of his faith". Martha also taught him news ways of thinking about women, marriage and relationships. Martha found a marriage partner for him.

Abdullahi felt that his church expected the man he was caring for "to simply adjust himself" which he did not readily do. Abdullahi is an outlier for this question. Having been a convert from Islam himself, Abdullahi advocates a more nuanced approach which is less radical than the "insider" approach by Mallouhi. He wants to initially use "less alien Christian vocabulary" in his theological reflections with converts. He emphasises a "staged theology", so that the "difficult doctrines" can be dealt with in later discussions. He contextualises the Bible and uses it to explain "similar" Christian concepts to Islamic concepts.

Luke ensured that the man he cared for had a love for Muslims, and importantly did not hold any bitterness in his heart towards them. He attended Luke's house group where he found Christian fellowship. Luke arranged for other Christians from the same ethnic background as this man to attend a meeting at the bishop's house, which made him feel "connected to a wider community of believers".

John's mentee had issues with the reality of the "culture of church". John states that this man "had high moral expectations of the church". He felt that the church should "stand out and be different from society", and he was not sure he was seeing this being exhibited.

Ayuba had to deal with the issue of forgiveness for the lady she was looking after. She had been hurt by her own community and Ayuba wanted her to find healing and be able to let go of the resulting pain. Ayuba took her to a few churches to see where she might be able to settle. Ayuba found it hard to explain new concepts such as "speaking in tongues" to this lady, which confused her when she saw this. Ayuba, who is a convert from Islam herself, feels that her approach is about "being Christ for the convert". She states "they need peace, love and knowing that God is present in their lives".

Stephen and his wife state they are "patient with converts, making sure that we do not turn people into test cases to learn from". As each situation arose Stephen would discuss it, allowing individuals to think things through for themselves. Stephen has himself developed courses for new believers. He stressed that finding a balance between structured approaches, as opposed to natural one-to-one engagement, is a hard one. Issues of forgiveness have arisen and Stephen has had to find ways through these from a biblical perspective. Stephen emphasises the aspect of a new relationship with God, and a full understanding of the concept of grace. As part of his Bible studies, he stresses the difference between the word of God in the Quran and the "eternal" word of God, namely Jesus. Stephen wants converts to reconnect to their old traditions, understanding the good that is in them and using these beneficial values in their lives. When converts can reconcile broken relationships with families, he encourages this.

Fifth question: *How did you accommodate cultural transitions for the convert?*

Peter's church has Pakistani and Arab congregations which are bilingual, and where the worship, prayer and sermons are in Arabic,

Urdu and English. The individuals he has looked after were encouraged to join these.

Esther's church has both Urdu and English congregations and the gentleman she looked after enjoyed being part of both. He did find the Christian way of praise and worship slightly alien at first, but later he came to enjoy it.

Mark's church was a unique example amongst those that I discovered. This multi-cultural church has always had focus of ministry to local Asians, with 80% of the congregation being South Asian. The services are in Asian languages as well in English. Mark's mentee received a lot of support from Pakistani Christian believers who had raised their own sons here. Mark did look for a marriage partner for the young man but to no avail.

Martha's church has Arabic, Chinese and Korean groups which meet in the church every week, and have prayer, worship and sermons in their own tongue. The individuals she looks after are encouraged to join these groups.

Luke's church has a mix of people from different ethnic backgrounds that the young man he looked after could relate to.

John was fortunate to get the man he looked after into an Anglican church that had services in Farsi, Urdu, Hindi and Punjabi, which the gentleman enjoyed. The church also had missionaries who had worked in Pakistan who could relate to him.

Ayuba did manage to find a church that the lady she was looking after was able to settle in. The congregation was full of Iranians, South Asians and Africans. Importantly, Ayuba felt the lady "was loved and accepted" by this church.

Stephen and his wife introduced the lady they were supporting to a Farsi congregation, which she enjoyed attending. In addition, she also came to their church, where the services were in English. The young man they looked after is investigating more about Asian Christian youth culture in the UK and has got connected to a group called "Naujavan", which promotes being distinctively Asian and Christian with all the cultural diversity and sensitivity which this requires.

Sixth question: *How are converts from Islam cared for by your church today?*

Peter's main aim is to train members of his own church to become the trusted Christians that converts would turn to for help.

Simon feels that a majority of churches in the UK have not fully understood what it takes to help converts from Islam. He feels that converts should "not be expected to just fit into our ways". Instead, they should retain their cultural identity and be used in this context to help future converts. Simon feels that there are issues to do with apostasy (*ridda*) and about how the Church uses the skills of converts, in mission and for helping new converts from Islam, that need discussion.

Mark's multi-cultural church have thought through how to care for Asian believers. They have carefully considered issues such as modest dress codes, not placing the Bible on the floor, cultural approaches between the sexes, and sensitivity to non-Halal foods and alcohol. They have "formalised nurture groups" for all those who have committed to following Jesus from other faiths. Mark has written courses for new believers himself, which are cited in the bibliography. They also have language-specific Bible study groups. Mark states "very few churches in the UK are truly multi-cultural integrated churches, such as this one". Mark highlighted that, when a believer wants their family to come to the church for a visit, the church "offers a culturally appropriate setting" for the guests. Recently they offered a "langar", which is a Sikh public food offering, to all who attended the church.

Martha regularly holds training for her church on Islam. She hopes that a group of individuals with a "heart for this ministry of caring for converts" will come out of this.

Abdullahi's church consists mostly of South Asians, and focuses on welcoming everyone, with an emphasis on fellowship and offering hospitality. Abdullahi attends "a by personal invitation only" home fellowship group which was set up 15 years ago to care for converts from Islam. Muslims from all over the UK, who want to learn about the Christian tradition, have also been carefully invited to this group.

Luke is starting a new course that he has developed for converts from Islam. As a busy church leader he wants to see that missionaries who are based in his parish are used more effectively.

Ayuba finds she is caring for converts from Islam but feels the church has to focus on equipping individuals for this task. She is impressed by how self-sufficient Iranian believers are, wishing other ethnic groups were like them.

Stephen gave a seminar to churches in his parish on the care of converts from Islam. He keeps a list of converts in his parish, ensuring that in each church there are at least three people taking care of them. Stephen annually invites converts from Islam from around the UK to a gathering, which has become a way of gaining a wider support network for converts. Some converts have a "low-key secret faith" and this gathering can be one of the only times they may have real fellowship with other Christians.

My seventh and final question: *What do you feel are the most important aspects in the care of converts?*

Peter feels that we need to "not place too many expectations on converts, ministering to them at their own pace and allowing God to work in their lives".

Simon feels that the worst form of care is one where "the convert becomes dependent on the person caring for them". He feels that they "must make their own decisions".

Mark feels that caring for the convert is about "keeping in step with the Holy Spirit, praying with the person you are caring for and making your love evident". Mark asks for Christians to exercise caution with whom they speak to about converts from Islam. Mark understands the responsibility that God has given Christians who care for converts; he quotes from the Bible, Luke 12:48: "From everyone who has been given much, much will be demanded; and for the one who has been entrusted with much, much more will be asked". Mark understands the costly hardship that converts face, having seen this for himself. He realises the pressure for converts to revert back to Islam, stressing that the church needs to remember the reality of this.

Martha feels converts need to know a "whole new family" of believers who will care for them. It is about a trusting commitment which requires Christians to come to their aid at times of difficulty and having a "bond of deep friendship".

Abdullahi states that the convert's discipleship path is about "embracing Christ, following Christ and the longer-term goal, which is about submitting to Christ". Caring for a convert involves being wholeheartedly there for them in this journey of commitment.

John states that caring for the convert is about giving the new believer "a sense of belonging". It is about "sharing in their joys, frustrations and sorrows". John states "sometimes churches can be very cold places". John feels "to welcome those of other faiths into churches in a way that makes them want to come back, is a key task for the church".

Ayuba asks for the "whole person" to be cared for, not just their "spiritual needs".

Stephen and his wife feel caring for a convert is about "holistic care and unconditional love". It is also about realising "the privilege that God has given Christians in seeing the spiritual walk of a new believer, with an involvement in their life."

Chapter Three – Analysing the Responses

Before presenting the analysis, I need to present three observations. First, we need to note key informant bias. This is when researchers rely on key informants for a major part of their final data, who may not be representative of the group as a whole, in the study. This could be the case for our candidates, as there are no current statistics to validate this against.

Secondly, we need to understand the realistic objectives of this study. This is to discover insights, qualitatively, from a small sample size that can realistically be used for guidance in the care of converts from Islam to Christianity. The objective is not to draw substantive conclusions that can be used to represent the care of all converts from Islam to Christianity nationally in the UK. This would require quantitative studies and probability sampling, which allows the precise extrapolation of results to defined populations. It would also require a wider spectrum of converts and those who care for them, from different denominations and ethnic backgrounds.

Thirdly, as we progress through the analysis, I will revisit my original challenging question. In this study, what is the level of understanding of identity issues amongst converts and those who care for them? I will also note observations that serve to answer this hypothesis, or an explanation of the phenomena observed. The hypothesis is that as a Muslim converts from Islam each is taken on a different "straight path" which, because it focuses on a personal relationship with Christ, embraces all the emotional, intellectual and cognitive highs and lows of any intense intimate relationship.

Key Moments in Conversion

The majority of the key moments in conversion in this study were based on the "relational", as converts meet with Christians and as they first encounter God in the text of the Bible. The converts have all felt a "sense of belonging" being important. For conversion to become "belonging", the converts need to re-encounter Christ repeatedly. God was faithfully near them in all they had been through. Eventually they found "peace", "truth" and a "special love" in Jesus. For born Christians, it can be surprising to see God directly taking the initiative in this way. Gaudeul states "it can be a sobering experience to find oneself before God's untamed freedom" (Gaudeul, 1999:244). Converts do need assistance to discern what has happened to them and whether their call was genuine; Christians should be there to help them do this (p245). These keymoment conversion observations underpin and emphasise my hypothesis: the intense highs of an intimate personal relationship with Christ.

In the convert's key faith journey moments, we see a number of important themes appear. Dreams become evident, a common "supernatural" phenomenon with God, for many Muslims. For rules on interpretation of these dream phenomena, the reader could consult *The Spiritual Exercises of Ignatius of Loyola* (Gaudeul, 1999:224). We see crises feature, from thoughts of suicide to depression, which frequently occur on the conversion journey. The converts experience the true cost of following Christ, in emotional distress, estrangement and violence. Dependency on God, and empowerment in the Holy Spirit, are expressed. Reaching into scripture, trying to find God's presence there, is articulated. These observations too, speak to my hypothesis that converts from Islam are taken on a different "straight path"; the intense psychological, emotional, intellectual and cognitive highs and lows, as the convert walks on their spiritual path with Christ.

"At Home in the Faith"

All the converts felt most at "home in the faith" when they were being loved, supported and, most importantly, were understood. Their stories speak about understanding their "new identities in Christ" and settling in these. A sense of feeling God and His Holy Spirit near them and knowing they had been strongly called to a "vocation" (Gaudeul, 1999:219). Gaudeul states "there is a certitude that God speaks to men [sic]. Christians believe the Spirit of God speaks to the heart of everyone" (Gaudeul, 1999:220).

I feel, from experience, that the convert from Islam undergoes several transitions before their "home" arrives, such as attraction, excitement, feeling deceived, loneliness, rejection, inner struggle, new self-awareness and finally settlement. I suggest that, here again, we observe the emotional and cognitive highs and lows related to an increased intense intimacy with Christ.

SUPPORT PROVIDED TO CONVERTS

In the area of support given to converts, we see some contrasts in the responses. Catholic converts go through a care approach that makes them feel part of an inclusive community and a family of believers very early on. All the converts naturally desire authentic care which fulfills their practical and emotional needs, not just focusing on the spiritual.

I argue that, when an "identity crisis" was taking place for Inaya, the churches struggled to help. In this instance we see a difference in cultural perception, hence why there was a conflict between Inaya's expectations and the help the Church needed to give. Moreover, in the West, people live in an individualistic culture which promotes personal autonomy, and this can be sometimes seen in the Western Church. In contrast, Muslims come from a "community-based culture", belonging to a supportive *Ummah* (brotherhood). The unity of the community, expressed in *Ummah*, is seen as a communal expression of *tawhid* (oneness of God), a foundational Islamic concept.

Phil Lewis, a Christian sociologist who writes on Islam in Britain, expresses an opposing view which suggests a rather tenuous brotherhood. He states "thus an 'emotional attachment' to the notion of belonging to a shared Muslim world – the '*Ummah*', does not transcend to residential segregation or to marriage within ethnically bonded groups" (Lewis, 2007:22). A fragile *Ummah* may well exist, and it may well be incorrect to place high expectations on the notion of a Christian equivalent. However, the converts in our study welcomed the mediation of the Church in resolving problems that they faced. The Church may need to question where their responsibilities should start and end, and what role they have to play in the aftermath of their witness to Muslims. I suggest that, in Inaya's case, we see a lack of understanding of identity issues by those who cared for her, even though Inaya did eventually understand what was happening.

DIFFICULTIES CONVERTS FACED

The difficulties that the converts faced were varied. 40% of converts had issues with settling into a church. These were attributed to struggles with identity, and lack of cultural understanding by churches, but other underlying factors could be present.

"Testimonies" and speaking to families about conversion are also stressed.

"Testimonies" are the accounts of how Christians come to faith in Christ. How converts prepare themselves in articulating these to Christians is an ongoing, multifaceted problem. Christians in each instance may need to think about whether the positive aspects of this type of witness outweigh the negative aspects for the convert, such as emotional distress, and infringement of their safety and privacy.

Concerns about when to tell their families about their conversion is an issue not handled well, and is also evident in the research carried out by T Walsh. A majority of the converts Walsh interviewed were never given any advice by the Church on this matter (Walsh, 2005:35).

I believe that, years ago when converts came to faith, they underwent an "extraction" from their cultural identities. Churches did not always understand the repercussions, but converts like Maryam have since expressed identity-related issues. Moreover, Chandler states "Muslims who decide to follow Christ all too often end up leaving their own culture and joining a "foreign one", a "Christian culture", dislocated from families and communities, losing their own identity and unable to influence the circle from which they originated" (Chandler, 2007:2).

I discovered three opposing arguments, according to theologians, for why converts do not lose their birth identities. Firstly, being part of Western culture does not equate to being a Christian. Secondly, following Jesus is not about following a religion, with a heritage, but about a relationship with God. Thirdly, the Christian faith cannot be identified with any one culture. "It is neutral to cultural practices such as what you eat, wear, your language and the things that make up most of your life" (Rasiah & Thomson, 2011:27).

I suggest that these observations clearly show that there is a lack of understanding of identity issues amongst those who care for converts. Moreover, the other aspect, often forgotten, is that the converts come from immigrant families, with some from mixed races. These cause further identity issues, producing increased schisms in the individual which must be healed, and this before any conversion identity issues have even been considered.

Transitions into the New Faith

The transitions into the new faith were rarely sudden; more typical was a gradual process. Some experienced a new "freedom in Christ" (Galatians 5:1), describing the transition as a form of "liberation". Again, we observe the highs of intimacy in the relationship with God, taking us back to the hypothesis.

Maryam remembered her attachment to "honour and shame" thinking as part of her transitional struggles, which are also related to her identity attachments. This thinking is not unique to Islam and is a cause of converts remaining secretive about finding Jesus. Lewis speaks about honour in the context of the *biraderi* sub-culture imported to the UK from Pakistan. He states "the reputation of the 'biraderi' must be protected at all costs. A scandal in one family can tarnish the honor of the whole clan" (Lewis, 2007:49).

I feel that Inaya's transitional issues are the symptoms of self-discovery to comprehend her real identity, feeling she is one of the few converts who have reasoned this out for herself and now understands it. She had a "tension" within her for many years, holding two ideologies together, until she finally settled into an acceptance of keeping some practices of her old tradition and bringing them into the new.

This "double belonging" concept has been discussed by thinkers such as Knitter and Cornille. Paul Knitter, an author on interreligious dialogue, develops his ideas in three stages. He firstly articulates the area he is struggling with in Christian belief, then he "passes over" to how the Buddhist might deal with this, and finally "he passes back" to reformulate what he has learnt from Buddhism to deepen his Christian belief (Knitter, 2009:21–22).

Knitter states, for example, that "Christian dualism has separated God from the world in a way that it cannot show how the two form a unity" (p26). Buddhists conversely stress non-duality and that, due to the interdependence of things, there cannot be a neat separation of ultimate reality from the world. Finally, he passes back, looking at "Imagining God as Inter Being and a connecting

Spirit, and the world evolving through Him, thereby creation cannot be something separate from the Creator" (p37). Knitter's Buddhist reflections do not take him away from being a Christian but instead increase his self-awareness.

Catherine Cornille, a scholar and writer on non-Christian sacred texts, describes "multiple belonging" for a Christian as "the encounter with other religions that is framed by one's primary religious identity. Only those beliefs are endorsed that are not in contradiction to the Christian faith, and the meaning of symbols and rituals that may be adopted is altered to fit the Christian doctrinal tradition" (Cornille, 2010:4).

Cornille states that "multiple belonging" can be more radical when the Christian not only understands the "other" through the Christian tradition's perspective, but when the Christian tradition is understood through the perspective of the "other" (p4). She describes this as "deeply confusing and spiritually unsettling". The point is not to stay static in two traditions but to transform one tradition through religious inspiration from the "other". Moreover, she states "Christians who have exercised multiple belonging" see it as a "means of self-understanding and to grow in faithfulness to the 'truth' which lies beyond the boundaries of any fixed identity and exclusive sense of belonging" (p6).

I have reflected on Inaya's journey, feeling she actually is someone who has comfortably become a Muslim follower of Jesus; an "insider" remaining within the Islamic culture, exhibiting "multiple belonging" as an expression of her religious identity.

THEOLOGY OF CONVERSION

The "theology of conversion" appeared to be the most difficult question to answer. Overall, the interviewees could not make clear distinctions between their basic theology and their theology of conversion. This is important to note as it highlights the centrality of the conversion experience as core to their theology. They, overall, defined it as an acceptance of the gift of "new life" by God's grace and the action of the Holy Spirit, which leads to a commitment to follow Jesus and a "transformed life". There was an emphasis on the concept of a "new relationship with God", negating the importance of joining a new tradition and thereby diluting the idea of apostasy.

A new relationship with God would be a radical thought for any Muslim. Gaudeul states "Islam admits no union with God, in life or in prayer, and no possibility of a personal knowledge of God" (Gaudeul, 1999:185). Again, I observe the personal relationship with God being stressed and thereby our hypothesis strengthened.

Adjustments to a New Reality

Adjustments to a new reality and what they could take or leave behind was another challenging question. No one was prescriptive of how untangling from an old tradition could be done, which highlights the difficult transitions converts have to realise. I feel this question is as much about whether identity and transitions in this are fully understood by those who care for converts. Identity is multifaceted, as we will discover, touching on many levels of an individual's reality, and so it is unsurprising that those questioned could not fully articulate the answer.

Dealing with hurt, bitterness and forgiveness were important aspects highlighted. I think that all these issues are to do with the convert journeying with God and how this close relationship is challenging the new disciples to confront these issues.

I did note that virtually all who care for converts answered this question by focusing on contextualised studies of the Bible and the Quran. I feel that our candidates were using the exercise of reading religious texts as a means to an end. Moreover, Michael Barnes SJ feels the reading of religious texts in relation to one another has to be thoughtfully discerned and has a much "deeper" significance than simply making it an exercise to achieve a goal. Barnes argues "there is always a danger that one community of faith manipulates the precious traditions of another to meet their own needs. Reading is a 'relational' act. To engage with a text, more especially when the text encapsulates the scriptural wisdom of a different community of faith, is to enter into relationship with what is the other" (Barnes, 2011:390).

Abdullahi, who is a convert from Islam himself, did bravely advocate a more nuanced reality transition which is not as radical as the "insider approach" of Mallouhi. Ayuba, who again is a convert from Islam, felt that her approach is more about "being Christ to the convert" rather than anything initially about theology. I argue that both these converts are focusing our attention away from structured approaches, such as those above, towards "relational" approaches, as well as appreciating how converts are going to handle their new identity transitions. It is evident here that the level of understanding of converts themselves of identity issues and their transitions is well developed; their personal experiences give them this edge.

The Accommodation of Cultural Transitions for Converts

The accommodation of cultural transitions for the converts did have similar themes. I visited Iranian fellowships and can confirm that they have a self-sufficient approach. Their established fellowships reside inside Western churches and have been like this for many years. However, I have noted that, over many years, South Asian converts from Islam have not come together in the same manner and the reasons for this can only be based on differences in the specific cultural and religious dynamics of these two ethnic groups, which are currently non-conclusive.

All of the observations of cultural transition accommodations highlight that identity issues, even if not articulated clearly, are gradually being understood by those who care for converts, and the practical implications are now being realised.

How the Pastoral Care of Converts is Conducted Today

How the pastoral care of converts is carried out today in churches shows exactly why care of convert guidelines are needed. Discipleship is the life-long commitment of a new believer to follow Jesus. Although a convert's discipleship path is about a personal journey of resolve and perseverance, the success or failure of this is partly dependent on the care given to converts in the various "Church scenarios" that present themselves in the UK.

The study highlighted that 40% of converts had difficulties settling into the "right" church. Each convert must not be "owned by" any one church; they should explore the wide spectrum of churches available to them, especially when the sheer variety is going to be new to them and may be confusing and daunting. Abdullahi and Simon highlighted the need for "culturally sensitive" environments for converts. I interviewed a convert from Islam who has been a pastor in his diocese for 40 years, and his main anxiety is that South Asian churches may lose support. Although groups like "Naujavan" (highlighted in this study) exist, he perceives a lack of need to remain "distinctively Asian" amongst future generations of Asian Christians in the UK.

The "exclusive" ex-Muslim home fellowships cited by Abdullahi will work well initially as support networks, but what if they only continued this way and never mixed with other ethnic groups? I understand that these fellowships do not have strong links to the established church and a wider community of believers, which could be helpful for the flourishing of their members (all converts) in the future.

I suggest that there are a number of options available for the future in which converts can thrive and grow. The truly integrated multi-cultural church approach adopted by Mark is one refreshing positive option to pursue. Another option is the empowerment and equipping of the established Church of England. I have visited emerging multi-cultural church movements such as the Sanctuary in Birmingham, cited by Walsh in his research (Walsh, 2005:50). These may become more prevalent in the twenty-first century, as British Asian Christians develop their own understanding of what "church" means for them.

I feel that all of these church scenarios are part of understanding the importance of cultural identity transitions for converts. The fact that they exist confirms that those who care for converts, and the converts themselves, are attempting to comprehend this area and placing this knowledge into practical approaches.

Ideals for the Pastoral Care of Converts

The important recommended ideals for the pastoral care of converts are to understand the serious responsibility of the task and develop a God-honouring lifestyle which gives credibility to the Gospel message: caring for the "whole" person and sharing in their lives completely and ensuring they are part of your lives also. A loving commitment to prayerfully walk close by and to ensure they are growing in step with Holy Spirit. Ensuring they have a "family of believers" around them. Allowing them to make their own decisions as well as their own mistakes and trusting them in these. Other key attributes are to be available, to listen, be patient, be non-judgmental, be realistic, allow reflective thinking and to trust. A thorough biblical understanding for the foundations of the Christian way of life are also considered important. Christians do not have all the right answers, at the right point in time, in each convert's journey: everyone is learning together. The important thing is that Christians note and pass on the lessons they have learnt.

Thoughts on My Research Methodology

I will now briefly describe the component of Maxwell's interactive model approach of validity. "Validity is a goal rather than a product, and it is also relative to the circumstances of the research" (Maxwell, 1996:86). One possible "validity threat" is that the researcher imposes their own meanings on answers rather than understanding the perspective of the interviewees. I sought to avoid this by using open-ended questions, not leading interviewees and allowing them to give full, contextual answers. Consequently, I did not allow their own feelings to influence the interviews, conscious of the "lens" through which they were viewing the study, and their motivations from their own experiences and research. All attempts were made to remain objective throughout the interviewing and data analysis processes.

In this study there are alternative explanations that could exist for the phenomena being seen. For example, I assumed that converts liked "culturally sensitive churches". However, the unfortunate alternative explanation could be that they never "fitted into" the established Western churches and needed to find another home. Moreover, I feel that this alternative explanation does have limited evidence. Trevor Barnes of the BBC interviewed Robin Thomson of South Asian Concern during 2012. Robin stated that "although there are around 75,000 Asian Christians in the UK, they are a minority within a minority. When Asian Christians first came here they felt they had to be part of English culture to be accepted as Christians, they were on the edge". Ram Gidoomal's statements are stronger: "when Asian Christians came here in the 1950s–60s they did not find welcoming Christian communities so they formed their own fellowships". My hope is that in a twenty-first century multi-cultural

Britain, the situation for new converts should have changed, but there is no certainty it has.

All studies inherently have "internal and external generalizations", and this study has elements of both. Does this study have any lack of external generalisation? The conclusions drawn from our observations for our candidates may not be representative of their respective external groups as a whole. However, there is "face generalization" for these groups; is there any reason *to not believe* that their accounts apply more generally? (Maxwell, 1996:97). I have used the observations seen in our study to validate the hypothesis and answer the original challenging question. Four outliers were noted, which are discussed in the final chapter. Furthermore, I have challenged the data by offering alternative explanations, being able to give evidence to support them.

Finally, I feel that, due to limited space, the study's observations have only touched upon themes and ideas that constitute a multifaceted bigger picture. I conclude that the hypothesis and the original challenging question are answered in the observations of the study. Each disciple's intimate journey with Christ, and everything that this relationship involves, is revisited a number of times. This confirms how my hypothesis is the answer to the phenomena observed. I argue that identity transitions during conversion are a difficult area to comprehend. When identity issues surface, they are not fully understood or managed well by those who care for converts. Converts themselves, however, know that something important is happening in their reality with regards to their sense of self, their relationships and their interactions with society around them. Nevertheless, over time, helped by new insights from converts, understanding of these complex reality shifts will continue to evolve through wider discourse. I trust that this book makes a contribution to this reality.

Chapter Four – Conversion and Identity

I will start this final chapter by outlining the theoretical framework for conversion and identity. Later, I will critique the "insider approach", reflecting on what it teaches Christians for the future. Finally, I will return to my hypothesis and original challenging question: what is the level of understanding of identity issues amongst converts and those who care for them?

"The wind blows wherever it pleases. You hear its sound, but you cannot tell where it comes from or where it is going. So it is with everyone born of the Spirit" (John 3:8). The stories in the New Testament of Jesus calling the disciples show that the choice to convert is one of the central Christian events. The Church Fathers speak about growing new senses, the "spiritual senses". In order for conversion to become "belonging", this initial moment of being brought to Christ must be repeated again and again. Communion is essentially a repetition of this event and a way to practise God's presence.

The convert from Islam, as we have seen, lives in an emotionally draining state, without the protective shielding of their family. In Muslim societies, conversion can result in excommunication. This is described as exile to the "outside" – the *dar al-harb* (world of war). All the converts in this study are effectively living in this "exiled state". They have committed apostasy (*ridda*), and their actions can carry severe consequences.

A highly comprehensive work on conversion has been carried out by Rambo. He states conversion in Christianity is "a radical call to reject evil and embrace a relationship with God through faith" (Rambo, 1996:5). He describes the stages in conversion as: Context – Crisis – Quest – Encounter (God and Christians) – Interaction (community) – Commitment – Consequences (p17). In my own study, and also in the MA thesis of Messenger (p15) and Walsh (pp 18–19), this stage of crisis prior to quest is borne out by converts' accounts. Conversion is dependent on a myriad of factors: the theological, sociological, psychological and cultural.

During the time of transition in conversion, converts from Islam are holding on to multiple religious and cultural concepts. The major ones are of *Ummah* (brotherhood) and unity as expressed by *tawhid* (Oneness of God), a foundational Islamic concept. There is a "tension" as they transition, struggling with these concepts and opposing concepts of self-autonomy and individualism expressed in Western society, and sometimes visible in the Western Church. "Western Christians do not always appreciate the binding to community for a convert from Islam and how it creates 'tensions' in their identity" (Kraft, 2007:129).

In Christian convert accounts like those of Bilquis Sheikh, author of *I Dared to Call Him Father*, we see Muslims encountering Christ, placing their trust in Him as the one God has chosen as a Saviour for mankind. Jesus has attracted them, fascinated them and spoken to them in a very direct way. D Harper argues this point in his MA thesis that in the Old Testament we see communities and nations turning to God, whereas the New Testament narratives are focused more on individuals turning to God (Harper, 2004:16).

I now want to turn to the concept of identity more precisely. There is a vast array of literature on this subject, with no one universally accepted definition of the term identity. Psychologists talk about "inner self", whilst anthropologists speak of it being a collective label marking out different groups (Green, 2012:2–3). Identity is not static and, crucially, evolves over time. Furthermore, it is affected by the fact that we no longer live in closed societies around the world. Although in some sense simplified, Tim Green outlines the three-level conceptualisation of the definitions of identity first explained by Hallahmi. The top layer is the collective identity used by groups, an *ascribed* identity such as nationality. The middle layer is the social identity which is a cluster of identities used by a group, *absorbed* by an individual through relationships. And finally, the bottom ego layer is the private and unconscious layer, the inner sense of "self" that formulates your worldview, your *achieved* identity where you are making your own choices (pp3–6).

Green quotes Rambo, stating conversion "is a radical form of identity transformation" (p7). Conversion according to Green thereby touches all these three levels. Firstly, the ego level is affected as the old self diminishes and the new comes alive. This is evidenced in the Bible when Paul states "the old has gone and the new has come" (2 Corinthians 5:17). Secondly, the social level is affected when a convert interacts with a new community of Christian believers. However, the converts can find themselves alone, secretly believing. Green suggests that this causes further complications and quotes from Berger that "in extreme cases one loses the sense of reality and identity" (Berger, 1990:22). Thirdly, the collective layer is affected when the convert is now seen as an apostate and social outcast by the Muslim community (Green, 2012:7–9).

To illustrate these levels, I suggest, in regard to a convert, that the "Muslim" collective identity can remain a convert's ethnic identification even if it is not a religious identity. For them, Islam, as a collective identity, can also still persist, even if it is no longer a creed. The need for loyalty to the group comes from this and is the reason why converts can have difficulties extracting themselves from all that they once were part of.

As part of our discourse on identity and transitions in identity at conversion, I will next critique the "insider approach". In the Introduction I outlined the thinking of Mallouhi, an advocate of the "insider approach". He describes some of his issues in his early Christian life as "deep internal struggles", "a profound crisis of identity". He felt as if he had to choose: hate Islam or love Christianity, even embrace Zionism. He obviously was losing his sense of identity and needed to find himself again and rest in his "true" identity (Chandler, 2007:104–107).

Many of the most vocal in the debate are Westerners. In general, they have questioned what cultural forms and meanings of the Islamic tradition can be accurately translated into Christian forms. Proponents of insider approaches wish to see converts living within their families and communities, whilst still in communion with Christian believers, in churches that use "insider" language, and contextualised, biblically permissible cultural and Islamic forms. The Westerners' concerns are about the authenticity of the Bible and avoiding syncretism, which involves the blending of traditions into one new system. Proponents note that the early Christians walked in step with the Holy Spirit, living within their communities and living the way Christ did.

I suggest that the "insider approach" is not a simple debate. Firstly, the discourse has failed to recognise that the Muslim communities worldwide are very divergent, complicated by regional variances in ethnicity, sect and politics. The approach therefore cannot be universally applied; it has to be adapted to each new context. Secondly, the converts from the Gentile and Jewish communities in the early Church also had to develop new ways of transitioning from their old tradition, and this transition in highly structured societies is not a straightforward one. Islam, likewise, impacts virtually every sphere of a Muslim's life and is a communal faith. Thirdly, we have seen parallel issues with "Messianic Jews", who were determined not to lose their Jewish identity, and have avoided joining Gentile churches. Missionaries are now being challenged to apply the Christian message to each new culture, because a faith will either be adapted to a new cultural context or become irrelevant (see Neely, 1995:4).

Furthermore, I argue that the "insider approach" needs careful reflection. It would have been useful to hear the stories of other converts such as Mallouhi in Chandler's book to see if they raised the same concerns over identity; however, we only have this one lone voice, which makes an analysis difficult to conduct. In addition to this, I agree that we do need to be mindful of accusations of mistranslations of the Bible and syncretism, whilst converts evolve new paradigms. Encouragingly, converts have started to develop their understandings of identity and religious belonging. Their various approaches, such as the "insider" movement, are managing to inform and widen the discourse. For these converts, Christ is walking on the Muslim road.

Future Research

I feel that there are some useful future research areas that emanate from our last discussion. Some questions to ask could be: how are "insiders" generally perceived by Muslims? How successful are "insiders" in speaking to Muslims about Christ and a new way of life? How widespread is the "insider approach" amongst converts from Islam in the Middle East and the West, and indeed anywhere else? How successful are "insiders" for bridging the understanding between Islam and Christianity?

Conclusion

I now return to our original challenging question: what is the level of understanding of identity issues amongst converts and those who care for them? I noted four key themes in my study; I will discuss two of them, as they address identity themes.

Inaya's "multiple belonging" was a problem for Christians to comprehend. Inaya now recognises that this is a central part of her new identity as a Christian; not an anomaly, but as part of who she really is. More Christians may see this type of religious belonging in future converts and will need to find appropriate ways to sensitively engage with this. Abdullahi, as a convert from Islam himself, was one of the only individuals to try a more nuanced approach in caring for converts from Islam. Although his thinking is not as radical as Mallouhi's "insider approach", he is moving beyond the current paradigms towards new ground and understands identity issues in a more nuanced way. In the future more converts may articulate similar views. Abdullahi's thinking is more aligned to the concept of "transformation not rupture". He wants to protect converts on a gradual journey of self-discovery. On further analysis, I believe that, although "multiple belonging" is viewed by theologians as being a phenomenon primarily in individuals exploring the freedom of religious transformation beyond fixed boundaries, it is finding an unexpected expression in the religious belonging and identities of converts as they journey with Christ on their spiritual paths.

So, returning to my original hypothesis. Firstly, I have suggested that the conversion and discipleship experience is different in the two traditions of Islam and Christianity. As part of the background reading for this study, I noticed that Kate Zebiri highlights that for British converts to Islam there is little mention of supernaturally significant spiritual experiences in their conversion discourse. This is supported by Goddard who highlights the fact that 50% of converts to Christianity expressed a supernatural encounter, whereas only 4% (3 of the 72 surveyed) converts to Islam mentioned this (Goddard, 1995:167, 169).

Secondly, during their discipleship path, converts to Islam are seeking to follow an ordered "straight path". They have submitted to God and effectively keep following this path by the rules laid down. Conversion to Islam is about the "rational", and adherence to reasoned guidance (Zebiri, 2008:40–41). However, Christian discipleship is a gradual path, sometimes lasting a whole lifetime, due to the "relationship with God" which can be problematic. Conversion is "relational". As a Christian makes their life-long commitment to follow Jesus, they are journeying on a different "straight path", one that is complex, as they journey with Christ. They experience all the psychological, emotional, cognitive and intellectual highs and lows, as we have seen in our study, associated with any intense intimate relationship. This is best expressed by Richard Peace when he writes, "without regeneration conversion is a human effort" (Peace, 1995:353). In Islam therefore, we see conversion as primarily about human effort, whereas in Christianity, conversion is about repairing what has been damaged and lost, with the human being ultimately reconciled to God.

GLOSSARY

apostasy	leaving Islam; formal disaffiliation from, abandonment of, or renunciation of a religion by a person
ridda	apostasy from Islam
tawhid	central theological concept of Islam stating that God is one
ummah	Islamic concept that all Muslims are part of one community; literally, brotherhood

Bibliography

Barnes, M. 2011. "Reading Other Religious Texts: Intratextuality and the Logic of Scripture." *Journal of Ecumenical Studies*, 46:3: 389–410.

Chandler, Paul. 2007. *Pilgrims of Christ on the Muslim Road.* UK, NY, Toronto: Rowman & Littlefield Publishers.

Cornille, Catherine. 2010. "The Dynamics of Multiple Belonging" in Cornille, Catherine (ed) *Many Mansions? Multiple Religious Belonging and Christian Identity*. Oregon: Wipf & Stock Publishers.

Gaudeul, J M. 1999. *Called from Islam to Christ – Why Muslims Become Christians*. UK: Monarch Books.

Gaudeul, J M. 1999. *The Spiritual Exercises of Ignatius of Loyola.*

Goddard, H. 1995. *Christians and Muslims: From Double Standards to Mutual Understanding*. London, NY: Routledge Curzon.

Green, T. 2012. "Conversion and Identity" in (ed) Greenlee, D, *Longing for Community: Church, Ummah or Somewhere in Between?* Pasadena, US: William Carey Library.

Harper, D. 2004. "Why South Asians in Britain Come to Christ: Factors in the Conversion to Christ of People of Other Faiths." MA thesis, All Nations Christian College. Unpublished.

Heider, E R. 1972. "Probability, Sampling, and Ethnographic Method: The Case of Dani Colour Names." *Man*, 7: 448–466.

Knitter, Paul. 2009. "Nirvana and God the Personal Other" in Knitter, Paul (ed) *Without Buddha I Could Not Be a Christian*. Oxford: Oneworld Publications.

Kraft, K A. 2007. "Community and Identity Amongst Arabs of a Muslim Background who Choose to Follow a Christian Faith." PhD thesis, University of Bristol. Unpublished.

Lave, C A & March, J G. 1975. *An Introduction to Models in the Social Sciences*. NY: Harper and Row.

Lewis, P. 2007. *Young, British and Muslim.* London: Continuum International.

Maxwell, J A. 1996. *Qualitative Research Design – An Interactive Approach.* Applied Social Research Methods Series, Vol 41. London: Sage Publications.

Messenger, T. 1999. "The Conversion of South Asian Muslims to Christianity in the UK." MA in Theology and Religious Studies thesis, University of Leeds. Unpublished.
Neely, A. 1995. *Christian Mission*. Maryknoll NY: Orbis Books.
Peace, R V. 1999. *Conversion in the New Testament*. Grand Rapids: Eerdmans.
Rambo, L. 1993. *Understanding Religious Conversion*. New Haven: Yale University Press.
Rasiah, C & Thomson, R. 2011. *Notes for the Journey – Following Jesus and Staying South Asian*. India: Horizon Printers.
Sankoff, G. 1971. "Quantitative Aspects of Sharing and Variability in a Cognitive Model." *Ethnology*, 10: 389–408.
Sheikh, Bilquis. 2003. *I Dared to Call Him Father* (special edition, first published 1978). Grand Rapids: Chosen Books.
Walsh, T. 2005. "Voices of Christians in Britain with a Muslim Background: Stories for the British Church on Evangelism, Conversion, Integration and Discipleship." MA in Mission Thesis, Birmingham Christian College. Unpublished.
Warraq, I. 2003. *Why I Am Not a Muslim*. Amherst, NY: Prometheus Books.
Zebiri, Kate. 2008. *British Muslim Converts – Choosing Alternative Lives*. Oxford: Oneworld Publications.